A NUMBER

by **Caryl Churchill**

Cast
Daniel Craig
Michael Gambon

Director **Stephen Daldry**
Designer **Ian MacNeil**
Costume Designer **Joan Wadge**
Lighting Designer **Rick Fisher**
Sound Designer **Ian Dickinson**
Assistant Director **Sarah Wooley**
Casting Director **Lisa Makin**
Production Manager **Paul Handley**
Stage Manager **Cath Binks**
Deputy Stage Manager **Rachel Claire Lovett**
Assistant Stage Manager **Helena Lane-Smith**
Costume Supervisors **Iona Kenrick, Jackie Orton**
Company Voice Work **Patsy Rodenburg**
Set construction **Souvenir Ltd**

Royal Court Theatre would like to thank the following for their help with this production:
Paul Kieve. Wardrobe care by Persil and Comfort courtesy of Lever Faberge.

THE COMPANY

Caryl Churchill (writer)
For the Royal Court plays include: Owners, Light Shining in Buckinghamshire, Cloud Nine, Top Girls, Fen (Joint Stock), Serious Money, Ice Cream, Mad Forest (Central School of Speech and Drama), Thyestes (translation from Seneca), This is a Chair, Blue Heart (Out of Joint), Far Away.
Other theatre includes: Vinegar Tom (Monstrous Regiment); Softcops (RSC); The Skriker (RNT); Lives of the Great Poisoners, Hotel (Second Stride).

Daniel Craig
Theatre includes: Angels in America (RNT) and Hurly Burly (Peter Hall Company).
Television includes: The Icehouse, Moll Flanders, Our Friends in the North.
Film includes: Tomb Raider, Some Voices, The Trench, Elizabeth I, Love is the Devil.
Awards include: Best Actor BIFA 2000 for Some Voices and Pathe British Performance Award at the Edinburgh Film Festival 1998 for Love is the Devil.
Daniel appears in Sam Mendes' latest film, The Road to Perdition.

Stephen Daldry (director)
Stephen is an Associate Director at the Royal Court. Director of the Royal Court 1998-2000. Artistic Director of the Royal Court 1993-98 and of the Gate Theatre, Notting Hill 1989-92.
For the Royal Court: Far Away, Via Dolorosa, This is a Chair, Body Talk, Rat in the Skull, The Kitchen, The Editing Process, Search and Destroy.
Other theatre includes: An Inspector Calls (RNT, West End, Broadway, international); Machinal (RNT); Damned for Despair, The Fleisser Plays (with Annie Castledine), Figaro Gets Divorced (Gate).
He directed the award-winning film Billy Elliot. His latest film The Hours is to be released in early 2003.

Ian Dickinson (sound designer)
For the Royal Court: Mother Teresa is Dead, Push Up, Workers Writes, F***ing Games, Herons, Cutting Through the Carnival.
Other theatre includes: Night of the Soul (RSC Barbican); Eyes of the Kappa (Gate); Crime and Punishment in Dalston (Arcola Theatre); Search and Destroy (New End, Hampstead); Phaedra, Three Sisters, The Shaughraun, Writer's Cramp (Royal Lyceum, Edinburgh); The Whore's Dream (RSC Fringe, Edinburgh); As You Like It, An Experienced Woman Gives Advice, Present Laughter, The Philadelphia Story, Wolks World, Poor Superman, Martin Yesterday, Fast Food, Coyote Ugly, Prizenight (Royal Exchange, Manchester); Great Monsters of Western Street (Throat Theatre Company); Small Craft Warnings, Tieble and Her Demon (Manchester Evening News Theatre Awards Best Design Team), The Merchant of Venice, Death and The Maiden (Library Theatre Company, Manchester).
Ian is Head of Sound at the Royal Court.

Rick Fisher (lighting designer)
For the Royal Court: Far Away, My Zinc Bed, Via Dolorosa(and Broadway), The Old Neighborhood, Fair Game, Hysteria, The Changing Room, Rat in the Skull (Royal Court Classics), King Lear, Six Degrees of Separation (also Comedy Theatre), A Mouthful of Birds, The Queen and I (also Vaudeville Theatre), Serious Money, Bloody Poetry, Three Birds Alighting on a Field.
Other theatre includes: Jerry Springer The Opera (Edinburgh Festival); Lobby Hero, A Boston Marriage (Donmar, New Ambassadors); A Russian in the Woods (RSC); The Glee Club (Duchess, Bush); Mother Clap's Molly House (RNT, Aldwych); Star Quality (Apollo); Afore Night Come (Young Vic); Napoleon (Shaftesbury); A Winter's Tale, Albert Speer, Blue/Orange, Widowers' Houses, Flight, Death of a Salesman, Machinal (RNT); An Inspector Calls (RNT, West End, Broadway, International); The Hunchback of Notre Dame (Berlin).
Dance includes: Swan Lake (Piccadilly/Los Angeles/Broadway), Cinderella (Piccadilly) - both for Adventures in Motion Pictures.
Opera includes: Clemenza di Tito, Traviata, Egyptian Helen, Wozzeck (Santa Fe); The Flying Dutchman (Spoleto Festival); La Vestale (English National Opera); Of Mice and Men (Washington); Verdi Requiem, Dr Ox's Experiment, Fairy Queen (ENO); Wozzek (Florence); Flying Dutchman (Bordeaux); Traviata (Paris Opera); Gloriana, Medea, La Boheme (Opera North).
Awards include: Olivier Award for Hysteria (Royal Court), Lady in the Dark, Chips with Everything, Machinal (RNT), Moonlight (Almeida); Tony Award for An Inspector Calls (Broadway).
Future projects include Turandot for the Bolshoi in Moscow and Wozzek for the Royal Opera House.

Michael Gambon
Theatre includes: Betrayal, Richard III, Othello, The Life of Galileo, Close of Play, Tales From Hollywood, Sisterly Feelings, A Chorus of Disapproval, A Small Family Business, Tons of Money, Mountain Language Volpone (RNT), A View From the Bridge (RNT, Aldwych), Skylight (RNT, Wyndham's Theatre, Broadway); King Lear, Antony and Cleopatra, (RSC) The Unexpected Man (RSC,

Duchess Theatre); Otherwise Engaged, The Norman Conquests, Just Between Ourselves, Man of the Moment, Alice's Boys, Uncle Vanya, Veterans Day, Old Times, Tom and Clem, Cressida, The Caretaker (West End).
Film includes: Sleepy Hollow, The Insider, The Gambler, Dancing at Lughnasa, Plunkett and Macleane, The Last September, The Cook, The Thief, His Wife and Her Lover, High Heels Low Lifes, End Game, Charlotte Gray, Gosford Park, Ali G The Movie, Path to War, The Actors, Open Range.
Television includes: The Singing Detective, Wives and Daughters, Longitude, Perfect Strangers.
Awards include: Theatre Critics' Award for The Life of Galileo, Olivier Award for A Chorus of Disapproval, all the major drama awards for A View From the Bridge in 1987, Evening Standard Best Actor Award for Skylight and Volpone (RNT), Olivier Award for Man of the Moment, Theatre Critics' Award for The Caretaker (West End), BAFTA Award, the Broadcasting Guild Award, Royal Television Society Award for The Singing Detective, BAFTA and Royal Television Society Best Actor Awards for Wives and Daughters, BAFTA Best Actor Awards for Longitude and Perfect Strangers. Michael Gambon was made a CBE in 1990, and was knighted in 1998.

Ian MacNeil (designer)
For the Royal Court: Plasticine, Far Away, Via Dolorosa (also Broadway and Duchess Theatre, West End), This is a Chair, Body Talk, The Editing Process, Death and the Maiden.
Other theatre includes: Afore Night Come (Young Vic); Albert Speer, Machinal (RNT); An Inspector Calls (RNT, West End, Broadway, international); The Ingolstadt Plays, Figaro Gets Divorced, Jerker (Gate); Enter Achilles, Bound to Please (DV8).
Opera includes: Medea (Opera North); Tristan and Isolde, Der Freischutz (ENO); Ariodante (ENO and Welsh Opera); La Traviata (Paris, Opera); Il Ritorno d'Ulisse in Patria (Munich Opera).
Film and television includes: Winterriese (Channel 4), Eight (Working Title), The Hours (Paramount, Associate Producer).
Awards include: Olivier Award for Best Opera for Tristan and Isolde, Critics' Circle Awards for Machinal and An Inspector Calls, Olivier Award for Design for An Inspector Calls, Best Design Tony nomination for An Inspector Calls, Broadway, Evening Standard Award nomination 2001 for Afore Night Come.
Design work for the music business includes set

and costume design for and the staging of several Pet Shop Boys world tours since 1999.

Joan Wadge (costume designer)
For the Royal Court: Plasticine.
Other theatre includes: Afore Night Come (Young Vic); Albert Speer (RNT)
Film and television includes: The Human Face, Adventures of the Worst Witch, Heaven on Earth, The Phoenix and the Carpet, The Lenny Henry Show, Ivanhoe, Henry IV, The Chamber, Ghost Story, The Great Kandinsky, The House of Eliott, The Adventures of Christopher Columbus, In Dreams, Old Times, Antonia and Jane- A Definitive Annual Report, Summer's Lease, All Passion Spent, The Interrogation of John.
Awards include: BAFTA nomination for Best Costume Design 1995 for Henry IV, EMMY Award 1994 for House of Eliott, BAFTA Award for Costume Design and EMMY nomination for House of Eliott.

Sarah Wooley (assistant director)
For the Royal Court as assistant director: The Trick is to Keep Breathing (Tron Theatre).
As Staff Director, theatre includes: Luther, Remembrance of Things Past, Romeo and Juliet (RNT).
As director, theatre includes: Departures (Old Vic); A Sexual Congress/Sladek (RNT Platforms) Venus and Adonis (Open Air Theatre, Regents Park); Thirteenth Night (Southwark Playhouse/Arches Theatre, Glasgow); Skinless (CCA); Sex, Drugs, Rock 'n' Roll (Tron Theatre Company); Scott of the Antarctic (Citizens Theatre, Glasgow); Talk Radio (Arches Theatre); Katie's Boys (Strathclyde Arts Centre); Kennedy's Children (Arches Theatre/Chandler Studio Theatre).
As assistant director, theatre includes: A Funny Thing Happened On The Way To The Forum, The Merry Wives of Windsor, Twelfth Night (Open Air Theatre, Regents Park); Sacco and Vanzetti, The Plaza, Endgame (Tron Theatre, Glasgow); The Merchant of Venice (Royal Lyceum, Edinburgh); Away (Traverse Theatre Company).

THE ENGLISH STAGE COMPANY AT THE ROYAL COURT

The English Stage Company at the Royal Court opened in 1956 as a subsidised theatre producing new British plays, international plays and some classical revivals.

The first artistic director George Devine aimed to create a writers' theatre, 'a place where the dramatist is acknowledged as the fundamental creative force in the theatre and where the play is more important than the actors, the director, the designer'. The urgent need was to find a contemporary style in which the play, the acting, direction and design are all combined. He believed that 'the battle will be a long one to continue to create the right conditions for writers to work in'.

Devine aimed to discover 'hard-hitting, uncompromising writers whose plays are stimulating, provocative and exciting'. The Royal Court production of John Osborne's Look Back in Anger in May 1956 is now seen as the decisive starting point of modern British drama and the policy created a new generation of British playwrights. The first wave included John Osborne, Arnold Wesker, John Arden, Ann Jellicoe, N F Simpson and Edward Bond. Early seasons included new international plays by Bertolt Brecht, Eugène Ionesco, Samuel Beckett, Jean-Paul Sartre and Marguerite Duras.

The theatre started with the 400-seat proscenium arch Theatre Downstairs, and then in 1969 opened a second theatre, the 60-seat studio Theatre Upstairs. Some productions transfer to the West End, such as Caryl Churchill's Far Away, Conor McPherson's The Weir, Kevin Elyot's Mouth to Mouth and My Night With Reg. The Royal Court also co-produces plays which have transferred to the West End or toured internationally, such as Sebastian Barry's The Steward of Christendom and Mark Ravenhill's Shopping and Fucking (with Out of Joint), Martin McDonagh's The Beauty Queen Of Leenane (with Druid Theatre Company), Ayub Khan-Din's East is East (with Tamasha Theatre Company, and now a feature film).

Since 1994 the Royal Court's artistic policy has again been vigorously directed to finding and producing a new generation of playwrights. The writers include Joe Penhall, Rebecca Prichard, Michael Wynne, Nick Grosso, Judy Upton, Meredith Oakes, Sarah Kane, Anthony Neilson, Judith Johnson, James Stock, Jez Butterworth, Marina Carr, Phyllis Nagy, Simon Block, Martin McDonagh, Mark Ravenhill, Ayub Khan-Din, Tamantha Hammerschlag, Jess Walters, Che Walker, Conor McPherson, Simon Stephens,

photo: Andy Chopping

Richard Bean, Roy Williams, Gary Mitchell, Mick Mahoney, Rebecca Gilman, Christopher Shinn, Kia Corthron, David Gieselmann, Marius von Mayenburg, David Eldridge, Leo Butler, Zinnie Harris, Grae Cleugh, Roland Schimmelpfennig and Vassily Sigarev. This expanded programme of new plays has been made possible through the support of A.S.K Theater Projects, the Jerwood Charitable Foundation, the American Friends of the Royal Court Theatre and many in association with the Royal National Theatre Studio.

In recent years there have been record-breaking productions at the box office, with capacity houses for Jez Butterworth's The Night Heron, Rebecca Gilman's Boy Gets Girl, Kevin Elyot's Mouth To Mouth, David Hare's My Zinc Bed and Conor McPherson's The Weir, which transferred to the West End in October 1998 and ran for nearly two years at the Duke of York's Theatre.

The newly refurbished theatre in Sloane Square opened in February 2000, with a policy still inspired by the first artistic director George Devine. The Royal Court is an international theatre for new plays and new playwrights, and the work shapes contemporary drama in Britain and overseas.

AWARDS FOR
THE ROYAL COURT

Terry Johnson's Hysteria won the 1994 Olivier Award for Best Comedy, and also the Writers' Guild Award for Best West End Play. Kevin Elyot's My Night with Reg won the 1994 Writers' Guild Award for Best Fringe Play, the Evening Standard Award for Best Comedy, and the 1994 Olivier Award for Best Comedy. Joe Penhall was joint winner of the 1994 John Whiting Award for Some Voices. Sebastian Barry won the 1995 Writers' Guild Award for Best Fringe Play, the Critics' Circle Award and the 1995 Lloyds Private Banking Playwright of the Year Award for The Steward of Christendom. Jez Butterworth won the 1995 George Devine Award, the Writers' Guild New Writer of the Year Award, the Evening Standard Award for Most Promising Playwright and the Olivier Award for Best Comedy for Mojo.

The Royal Court was the overall winner of the 1995 Prudential Award for the Arts for creativity, excellence, innovation and accessibility. The Royal Court Theatre Upstairs won the 1995 Peter Brook Empty Space Award for innovation and excellence in theatre.

Michael Wynne won the 1996 Meyer-Whitworth Award for The Knocky. Martin McDonagh won the 1996 George Devine Award, the 1996 Writers' Guild Best Fringe Play Award, the 1996 Critics' Circle Award and the 1996 Evening Standard Award for Most Promising Playwright for The Beauty Queen of Leenane. Marina Carr won the 19th Susan Smith Blackburn Prize (1996/7) for Portia Coughlan. Conor McPherson won the 1997 George Devine Award, the 1997 Critics' Circle Award and the 1997 Evening Standard Award for Most Promising Playwright for The Weir. Ayub Khan-Din won the 1997 Writers' Guild Awards for Best West End Play and Writers' Guild New Writer of the Year and the 1996 John Whiting Award for East is East (co-production with Tamasha).

At the 1998 Tony Awards, Martin McDonagh's The Beauty Queen of Leenane (co-production with Druid Theatre Company) won four awards including Garry Hynes for Best Director and was nominated for a further two. Eugene Ionesco's The Chairs (co-production with Theatre de Complicite) was nominated for six Tony awards. David Hare won the 1998 Time Out Live Award for Outstanding Achievement and six awards in New York including the Drama League, Drama Desk and New York Critics Circle Award for Via Dolorosa. Sarah Kane won the 1998 Arts Foundation Fellowship in Playwriting. Rebecca Prichard won the 1998 Critics' Circle Award for Most Promising Playwright for Yard Gal (co-production with Clean Break).

Conor McPherson won the 1999 Olivier Award for Best New Play for The Weir. The Royal Court won the 1999 ITI Award for Excellence in International Theatre. Sarah Kane's Cleansed was judged Best Foreign Language Play in 1999 by Theater Heute in Germany. Gary Mitchell won the 1999 Pearson Best Play Award for Trust. Rebecca Gilman was joint winner of the 1999 George Devine Award and won the 1999 Evening Standard Award for Most Promising Playwright for The Glory of Living.

In 1999, the Royal Court won the European theatre prize New Theatrical Realities, presented at Taormina Arte in Sicily, for its efforts in recent years in discovering and producing the work of young British dramatists.

Roy Williams and Gary Mitchell were joint winners of the George Devine Award 2000 for Most Promising Playwright for Lift Off and The Force of Change respectively. At the Barclays Theatre Awards 2000 presented by the TMA, Richard Wilson won the Best Director Award for David Gieselmann's Mr Kolpert and Jeremy Herbert won the Best Designer Award for Sarah Kane's 4.48 Psychosis. Gary Mitchell won the Evening Standard's Charles Wintour Award 2000 for Most Promising Playwright for The Force of Change. Stephen Jeffreys' I Just Stopped by to See The Man won an AT&T: On Stage Award 2000. David Eldridge's Under the Blue Sky won the Time Out Live Award 2001 for Best New Play in the West End. Leo Butler won the George Devine Award 2001 for Most Promising Playwright for Redundant. Roy Williams won the Evening Standard's Charles Wintour Award 2001 for Most Promising Playwright for Clubland. Grae Cleugh won the 2001 Olivier Award for Most Promising Playwright for Fucking Games.

ROYAL COURT BOOKSHOP

The bookshop offers a wide range of playtexts and theatre books, with over 1,000 titles. Located in the downstairs Bar and Food area, the bookshop is open Monday to Saturday, afternoons and evenings.

Many Royal Court playtexts are available for just £2 including works by Harold Pinter, Caryl Churchill, Rebecca Gilman, Martin Crimp, Sarah Kane, Conor McPherson, Ayub Khan-Din, Timberlake Wertenbaker and Roy Williams.

For information on titles and special events, Email: bookshop@royalcourttheatre.com
Tel: 020 7565 5024

REBUILDING THE ROYAL COURT

In 1995, the Royal Court was awarded a National Lottery grant through the Arts Council of England, to pay for three quarters of a £26m project to completely rebuild its 100-year old home. The rules of the award required the Royal Court to raise £7.6m in partnership funding. The building has been completed thanks to the generous support of those listed below.

We are particularly grateful for the contributions of over 5,700 audience members.

English Stage Company Registered Charity number 231242.

THE AMERICAN FRIENDS OF THE ROYAL COURT THEATRE

AFRCT support the mission of the Royal Court and are primarily focused on raising funds to enable the theatre to produce new work by emerging American writers. Since this not-for-profit organisation was founded in 1997, AFRCT has contributed to nine productions They have also supported the participation of young artists in the Royal Court's acclaimed International Residency.

If you would like to support the ongoing work of the Royal Court, please contact the Development Department on 020 7565 5050.

THE ARTS COUNCIL OF ENGLAND

PROGRAMME SUPPORTERS

The Royal Court (English Stage Company Ltd) receives its principal funding from London Arts. It is also supported financially by a wide range of private companies and public bodies and earns the remainder of its income from the box office and its own trading activities.

The Royal Borough of Kensington & Chelsea gives an annual grant to the Royal Court Young Writers' Programme and the Affiliation of London Government provides project funding for a number of play development initiatives.

The Jerwood Charitable Foundation continues to support new plays by new playwrights through the Jerwood New Playwrights series. Since 1993 the A.S.K. Theater Projects of Los Angeles has funded a Playwrights' Programme at the theatre. Bloomberg Mondays, the Royal Court's reduced price ticket scheme, is supported by Bloomberg. Over the past seven years the BBC has supported the Gerald Chapman Fund for directors.

TRUSTS AND FOUNDATIONS
American Friends of the Royal Court Theatre
A.S.K Theater Projects
The Carnegie United Kingdom Trust
Carlton Television Trust
Gerald Chapman Fund
The Foundation for Sport and the Arts
Genesis Foundation
The Goldsmiths' Company
The Haberdashers' Company
Paul Hamlyn Foundation
Jerwood Charitable Foundation
John Lyon's Charity
The Mercers' Company
The Laura Pels Foundation
Quercus Charitable Trust
The Peggy Ramsay Foundation
The Eva & Hans K Rausing Trust
The Royal Victoria Hall Foundation
The Peter Jay Sharp Foundation
The Sobell Foundation
The Trusthouse Charitable Foundation
Garfield Weston Foundation

MAJOR SPONSORS
American Airlines
Amerada Hess
BBC
Bloomberg
Channel Four
Lever Fabergé
Royal College of Psychiatrists

BUSINESS MEMBERS
Aviva plc
BP
Lazard
McCann-Erickson
Pemberton Greenish
Peter Jones
Redwood
Siemens
Simons Muirhead & Burton

PRODUCTION SYNDICATE
Anon
Jonathan & Sindy Caplan
Richard & Susan Hayden
William & Hilary Russell

INDIVIDUAL MEMBERS
Patrons
Anon
Advanpress
Mark Bentley
Mrs Alan Campbell-Johnson
Coppard & Co.
Mrs Phillip Donald
Robyn Durie
Tom & Simone Fenton
Ralph A Fields
Edna & Peter Goldstein
Homevale Ltd
Tamara Ingram
Mr & Mrs Jack Keenan
Barbara Minto
New Penny Productions Ltd
Martin Newson
AT Poeton & Son Ltd.
Caroline Quentin
William & Hilary Russell
Ian & Carol Sellars
Jan & Michael Topham
Amanda Vail

Benefactors
Anon
Anastasia Alexander
Lesley E Alexander
Mr & Mrs J Attard-Manché
Matilde Attolico
Tom Bendhem
Emma Bleasdale
Jasper Boersma
Keith & Helen Bolderson
Jeremy Bond
Eleanor Bowen
Brian Boylan
Katie Bradford
Julian Brookstone
Ossi & Paul Burger
Debbi & Richard Burston
Danielle Byrne
Yuen-Wei Chew
Martin Cliff

Carole & Neville Conrad
Barry Cox
Peter Czernin
David Day
Chris & Jane Deering
Zöe Dominic
Winston & Jean Fletcher
Charlotte & Nick Fraser
Jacqueline & Jonathan Gestetner
Michael Goddard
Carolyn Goldbart
Judy & Frank Grace
Byron Grote
Sue & Don Guiney
Amanda Howard Associates
Mrs Martha Hummer Bradley
Mr & Mrs T Kassem
Peter & Maria Kellner
Diana King
Lee & Thompson
Carole A Leng
Lady Lever
Colette & Peter Levy
Ann Lewis
Ian Mankin
Christopher Marcus
David Marks
Alan & Tricia Marshall
Nicola McFarland
Eva Monley
Pat Morton
Georgia Oetker
Paul Oppenheimer
Janet & Michael Orr
Maria Peacock
Jeremy Priestly
Simon Rebbechi
John & Rosemarie Reynolds
Kate Richardson
Samuel French Ltd
Bernice & Victor Sandelson
John Sandoe (Books) Ltd
Nicholas Selmes
Bernard Shapero
Jenny Sheridan
Lois Sieff OBE
Peregrine Simon
Brian D Smith
John Soderquist

The Spotlight
Anthony Wigram
Thai Ping Wong
George & Moira Yip
Georgia Zaris

ASSOCIATES
Mrs Elly Brook JP
Barry Cox
Phil Hobbs
Pauline Pinder
Sue Stapely
Carl & Martha Tack

STAGE HANDS CIRCLE
Graham Billing
Andrew Cryer
Lindy Fletcher
Susan Hayden
Mr R Hopkins
Philip Hughes Trust
Dr A V Jones
Roger Jospe
Miss A Lind-Smith
Mr J Mills
Nevin Charitable Trust
Janet & Michael Orr
Jeremy Priestley
Ann Scurfield
Brian Smith
Harry Streets
Thai Ping Wong
Richard Wilson OBE
C C Wright

NT National Theatre
Box Office 020 7452 3000

DINNER

by Moira Buffini

"It's my creation – like Frankenstein's monster."
Let the dinner from hell begin...

This is Moira Buffini's first play at the National - her previous
work includes *Loveplay* (RSC) and *Gabriel* (Soho Theatre).
It is directed by Fiona Buffini making a welcome return to
the National where she most recently directed *Playboy
of the Western World* in the Cottesloe.

Director Fiona Buffini, *Designer* Rachel Blues, *Sound Designer* Rich Walsh
Cast includes Nicholas Farrell, Harriet Walter

Reg'd Charity

Loft Theatre. Previews from 14 November. Opening 18 November
BOOKING OPENS 7 OCTOBER www.nationaltheatre.org.uk

THE ARTS COUNCIL OF ENGLAND

A NUMBER

Caryl Churchill

Characters

SALTER, *a man in his early sixties*

BERNARD, *his son, forty*

BERNARD, *his son, thirty-five*

MICHAEL BLACK, *his son, thirty-five*

The play is for two actors. One plays Salter, the other his sons.

The scene is the same throughout, it's where Salter lives.

1

SALTER, *a man in his early sixties and his son* BERNARD
(B2), *thirty-five.*

B2	A number
SALTER	you mean
B2	a number of them, of us, a considerable
SALTER	say
B2	ten, twenty
SALTER	didn't you ask?
B2	I got the impression
SALTER	why didn't you ask?
B2	I didn't think of asking.
SALTER	I can't think why not, it seems to me it would be the first thing you'd want to know, how far has this thing gone, how many of these things are there?
B2	Good, so if it ever happens to you
SALTER	no you're right
B2	no it was stupid, it was shock, I'd known for a week before I went to the hospital but it was still

SALTER   it is, I am, the shocking thing is that there *are* these, not how many but at all

B2   even one

SALTER   exactly, even one, a twin would be a shock

B2   a twin would be a surprise but a number

SALTER   a number any number is a shock.

B2   You said things, these things

SALTER   I said?

B2   you called them things. I think we'll find they're people.

SALTER   Yes of course they are, they are of course.

B2   Because I'm one.

SALTER   No.

B2   Yes. Why not? Yes.

SALTER   Because they're copies

B2   copies? they're not

SALTER   copies of you which some mad scientist has illegally

B2   how do you know that?

SALTER   I don't but

B2   what if someone else is the one, the first one, the real one and I'm

SALTER   no because

B2   not that I'm *not* real which is why I'm
            saying they're not things, don't call them

SALTER   just wait, because I'm your father.

B2   You know that?

SALTER   Of course.

B2   It was all a normal, everything, birth

SALTER   you think I wouldn't know if I wasn't
            your father?

B2   Yes of course I was just for a moment
            there, but they are all still people like
            twins are all, quins are all

SALTER   yes I'm sorry

B2   we just happen to have identical be
            identical identical genetic

SALTER   sorry I said things, I didn't mean
            anything by that, it just

B2   no forget it, it's nothing, it's

SALTER   because of course for me you're the

B2   yes I know what you meant, I just,
            because of course I want them to be
            things, I do think they're things, I don't
            think they're, of course I *do* think they're
            them just as much as I'm me but I. I
            don't know what I think, I feel terrible.

SALTER   I wonder if we can sue.

B2	Sue? who?
SALTER	Them, whoever did it. Who did you see?
B2	Just some young, I don't know, younger than me.
SALTER	So who did it?
B2	He's dead, he was some old and they've just found the records and they've traced
SALTER	so we sue the hospital.
B2	Maybe. Maybe we can.
SALTER	Because they've taken your cells
B2	but when how did they?
SALTER	when you were born maybe or later you broke your leg when you were two you were in the hospital, some hairs or scrapings of your skin
B2	but they didn't damage
SALTER	but it's you, part of you, the value
B2	the value of those people
SALTER	yes
B2	and what is the value of
SALTER	there you are, who knows, priceless, and they belong
B2	no
SALTER	they belong to you, they should belong to you, they're made from your

B2   they should

SALTER   they've been stolen from you and you
            should get your rights

B2   but is it

SALTER   what? is it money? is it something you
            can put a figure on? put a figure on it.

B2   This is purely

SALTER   yes

B2   suppose each person was worth ten
            thousand pounds

SALTER   a hundred

B2   a hundred thousand?

SALTER   they've taken a person away from you

B2   times the number of people

SALTER   which we don't know

B2   but a number a fairly large say anyway
            ten

SALTER   a million is the least you should take, I
            think it's more like half a million each
            person because what they've done
            they've damaged your uniqueness,
            weakened your identity, so we're looking
            at five million for a start.

B2   Maybe.

SALTER   Yes, because how dare they?

B2   We'd need to be able to prove

SALTER   we prove you're genetically my son
              genetically and then

B2   because there's no doubt

SALTER   no doubt at all. I suppose you didn't see
              one?

B2   One what? of them?

SALTER   of these people

B2   no I think they'd keep us apart wouldn't
              they so we don't spoil like contaminate
              the crime scene so you don't tell each
              other I have nightmares oh come to
              think of it I have nightmares and he
              might have said no if he was asked in
              the first place

SALTER   because they need to find out

B2   yes how much we're the same, not just
              how tall we are or do we get asthma but
              what do you call your dog, why did you
              leave your wife you don't even know the
              answer to these questions.

SALTER   So you didn't suddenly suddenly see

B2   what suddenly see myself coming round
              the corner

SALTER   because that could be

B2   like seeing yourself on the camera in a
              shop or you hear yourself on the

answering machine and you think god is
that what I

SALTER   but more than that, it'd be it'd be

B2   don't they say you die if you meet
             yourself?

SALTER   walk round the corner and see yourself
             you could get a heart attack. Because if
             that's me over there who am I?

B2   Yes but it's not me over there

SALTER   no I know

B2   it's like having a twin that's all it's just

SALTER   I know what it is.

B2   I think I'd like to meet one. It's an
             adventure isn't it and you're part of
             science. I wouldn't be frightened to meet
             any number.

SALTER   I don't know.

B2   They're all your sons.

SALTER   I don't want a number of sons, thank
             you, you're plenty, I'm fine.

B2   Maybe after they've found everything out
             they'll let us meet. They'll have a party
             for us, we can

SALTER   I'm not going to drink with those
             doctors. But maybe you're right you're
             right, take it in a positive spirit.

B2	There is a thing
SALTER	what's that?
B2	a thing that puzzles me a little
SALTER	what's that?
B2	I did get the impression and I know I may be wrong because maybe I was in shock but I got the impression there was this batch and we were all in it. I was in it.
SALTER	No because you're my son.
B2	No but we were all
SALTER	I explained already
B2	but I wasn't being quite open with you because I'm confused because it's a shock but I want to know what happened
SALTER	they stole
B2	no but what happened
SALTER	I don't
B2	because they said that none of us was the original.
SALTER	They said that?
B2	I think
SALTER	I think you're mistaken because you're confused
B2	you think

SALTER   you need to get back to them

B2   well I'll do that. But I think that's what they meant

SALTER   it's not what they meant

B2   ok. But that's my impression, that none of us is the original.

SALTER   Then who? do they know?

B2   they're not saying, they just say we were all

SALTER   they're not saying?

B2   so if I was your son the original would be your son too which is nonsense so

SALTER   does that follow?

B2   so please if you're not my father that's fine. If you couldn't have children or my mother, and you did in vitro or I don't know what you did I really think you should tell me.

SALTER   Yes, that's what it was.

B2   That's all right.

SALTER   Yes I know.

B2   Thank you for telling me.

SALTER   Yes.

B2   It's better to know.

SALTER   Yes.

B2   So don't be upset.

SALTER   No.

B2   You are though

SALTER   Well.

B2   I'm fine about it. I'm not quite sure
             what I'm fine about. There was some
             other person this original some baby or
             cluster or and there were a number a
             number of us made somehow and you
             were one of the people who acquired,
             something like that.

SALTER   It wasn't

B2   don't worry

SALTER   because the thing is you see that isn't
             what happened. I am your father, it was
             by an artificial the forefront of science
             but I am genetically.

B2   That's great.

SALTER   Yes.

B2   So I know the truth and you're still my
             father and that's fine.

SALTER   Yes.

B2   So what about this original? I don't quite
             I don't

SALTER   There was someone.

B2   There was what kind of someone?

SALTER   There was a son.

B2   A son of yours?

SALTER   Yes.

B2   So when was that?

SALTER   That was some time earlier.

B2   Some time before I was born there was

SALTER   another son, yes, a first

B2   who what, who died

SALTER   who died, yes

B2   and you wanted to replace him

SALTER   I wanted

B2   instead of just having another child you
           wanted

SALTER   because your mother was dead too

B2   but she died when I was born, I thought
           she

SALTER   well I'm telling you what happened.

B2   So what happened?

SALTER   So they'd been killed in a carcrash and

B2   my mother and this

SALTER   carcrash

B2   when was this? how old was the child,
           was he

SALTER   four, he was four

B2   and you wanted him back

SALTER   yes

B2   so I'm just him over again.

SALTER   No but you are you because that's who
            you are but I wanted one just the same
            because that seemed to me the most
            perfect

B2   but another child might have been better

SALTER   no I wanted the same

B2   but I'm not him

SALTER   no but you're just the way I wanted

B2   but I could have been a different person
            not like him I

SALTER   how could you? if I'd had a different
            child that wouldn't be you, would it.
            You're this one.

B2   I'm just a copy. I'm not the real one.

SALTER   You're the only one.

B2   What do you mean only, there's all the
            others, there's

SALTER   but I didn't know that, that wasn't part
            of the deal. They were meant to make
            one of you not a whole number, they
            stole that, we'll deal with, it's something
            for lawyers. But you're what I wanted,
            you're the one.

B2   Did you give me the same name as him?

SALTER   Does it make it worse?

B2   Probably.

2

SALTER *and his other son* BERNARD (B1), *forty.*

SALTER   So they stole – don't look at me – they
          stole your genetic material and

B1   no

SALTER   they're the ones you want to

B1   no

SALTER   because what ten twenty twenty copies of
          you walking round the streets

B1   no

SALTER   which was nothing to do with me
          whatsoever and I think you and I should
          be united on this.

B1   Let me look at you.

SALTER   You've been looking at me all the

B1   let me look at you.

SALTER   Bit older.

B1   No because your father's not young
          when you're small is he, he's not any
          age, he's more a power. He's a dark dark
          power which is why my heart, people
          pay trainers to get it up to this speed,
          but is it because my body recognises or

because I'm told? because if I'd seen you
in the street I don't think I'd've stopped
and shouted Daddy. But you'd've known
me wouldn't you. Unless you thought I
was one of the others.

SALTER   It's a long time.

B1   Can we talk about what you did?

SALTER   Yes of course. I'm not sure where what

B1   about you sent me away and had this
other one made from some bit of my
body some

SALTER   it didn't hurt you

B1   what bit

SALTER   I don't know what

B1   not a limb, they clearly didn't take a
limb like a starfish and grow

SALTER   a speck

B1   or half of me chopped through like a
worm and grow the other

SALTER   a scraping cells a speck a speck

B1   a speck yes because we're talking that
microscope world of giant blobs and
globs

SALTER   that's all

B1   and they take this painless scrape this
specky little cells of me and kept that
and you threw the rest of me away

SALTER   no

B1   and had a new one made

SALTER   no

B1   yes

SALTER   yes

B1   yes

SALTER   yes of course, you know I did, I'm not
              attempting to deny, I thought it was the
              best thing to do, it seemed a brilliant it
              was the only

B1   brilliant?

SALTER   it seemed

B1   to get rid

SALTER   it wasn't perfect. It was the best I could
              do, I wasn't very I was I was always and
              it's a blur to be honest but it was I
              promise you the best

B1   and this copy they grew of me, that
              worked out all right?

SALTER   There were failures of course, inevitable

B1   dead ones

SALTER   in the test tubes the dishes, I was told
              they didn't all

B1   but they finally got a satisfactory a
              bouncing

SALTER   yes but they lied to me because they didn't tell me

B1   in a cradle

SALTER   all those others, they stole

B1   and he looked just like me did he indistinguishable from

SALTER   yes

B1   so it worked out very well. And this son lives and breathes?

SALTER   yes

B1   talks and fucks? eats and walks? swims and dreams and exists somewhere right now yes does he? exist now?

SALTER   yes

B1   still exists

SALTER   yes of course

B1   happily?

SALTER   well mostly you could say

B1   as happily as most people?

SALTER   yes I think

B1   because most people are happy I read in the paper. Did it cost a lot of money?

SALTER   the procedure? to get?

B1   the baby

SALTER   yes.

B1   Were we rich?

SALTER   Not rich.

B1   No, I don't remember anything rich. A
              lot of dust under the bed those heaps of
              fluff you get don't you if you look if you
              go under there and lie in it.

SALTER   No, we weren't. But I managed. I was
              spending less.

B1   You made an effort.

SALTER   I did and for that money you'd think I'd
              get exclusive

B1   they ripped you off

SALTER   because one one was the deal and they

B1   what do you expect?

SALTER   from you too they it's you they, just so
              they can do some scientific some
              research some do you get asthma do you
              have a dog what do you call it do you

B1   Who did you think it was at the door?
              did you think it was one of the others or
              your son or

SALTER   I don't know the others

B1   you know your son

SALTER   I know

B1   your son the new

SALTER   yes of course

B1   you know him

SALTER   yes I wouldn't think he was you, no.

B1   You wouldn't think it was him having a bad day.

SALTER   You look very well.

B1   But it could have been one of the others?

SALTER   Yes because that's what I was thinking about, how could the doctors, I think there's money to be made out of this.

B1   I've not been lucky with dogs. I had this black and tan bitch wouldn't do what it's told, useless. Before that I had a lurcher they need too much running about. Then a friend of mine went inside could I look after, battle from day one with that dog, rottweiler pit bull I had to throw a chair, you could hit it with a belt it kept coming back. I'd keep it shut up in the other room and it barks so you have to hit it, I was glad when it bit a girl went to pat it and straight off to the vet, get rid of this one it's a bastard. My friend wasn't pleased but he shouldn't have gone in the postoffice.

SALTER   No that's right. I've never wanted a dog.

B1   Don't patronise me

SALTER   I'm not I'm not

B1   you don't know what you're doing

SALTER   I just

B1   because you go in a pub someone throws
his beer in your face you're supposed to
say sorry, he only had three stitches I'm
a very restrained person. Because this
minute we sit here there's somebody a lot
of them but think of one on the electric
bedsprings or water poured down his
throat and jump on his stomach. There's
a lot of wicked people. So that's why.
And you see them all around you. You
go down the street and you see their
faces and you think you don't fool me
I know what you're capable of. So don't
start anything.

SALTER   I think what we need is a good solicitor.

B1   What I like about a dog it stops people
getting after you, they're not going to
come round in the night. But they make
the place stink because I might want to
stay out a few days and when I get back
I might want to stay in a few days and
a dog can become a tyrant to you.

Silence.

Hello daddy daddy daddy, daddy hello.

SALTER   Nobody regrets more than me the
completely unforeseen unforeseeable
which isn't my fault and does make it
more upsetting but what I did did seem
at the time the only and also it's a
tribute, I could have had a different one,
a new child altogether that's what most

people but I wanted you again because I thought you were the best.

B1   It wasn't me again.

SALTER   No but the same basic the same raw materials because they were perfect. You were the most beautiful baby everyone said. As a child too you were very pretty, very pretty child.

B1   You know when I used to be shouting.

SALTER   No.

B1   When I was there in the dark. I'd be shouting.

SALTER   No.

B1   Yes, I'd be shouting dad dad

SALTER   Was this some time you had a bad dream or?

B1   shouting on and on

SALTER   I don't think I

B1   shouting and shouting

SALTER   no

B1   and you never came, nobody ever came

SALTER   so was this after your mum

B1   after my mum was dead this was after

SALTER   because you were very little when she

B1   yes because I can only remember

SALTER   you were maybe two when she

B1   and I remember her sitting there, she
            was there

SALTER   you remember so early?

B1   she'd be there but she wouldn't help stop
            anything

SALTER   I'm surprised

B1   so when I was shouting what I want to
            know

SALTER   but when was this

B1   I want to know if you could hear me or
            not because I never knew were you
            hearing me and not coming or could you
            not hear me and if I shouted loud
            enough you'd come

SALTER   I can't have heard you, no

B1   or maybe there was no one there at all
            and you'd gone out so no matter how
            hard I shouted there was no one there

SALTER   no that wouldn't have

B1   so then I'd stop shouting but it was
            worse

SALTER   because I hardly ever

B1   and I didn't dare get out of bed to go
            and see

SALTER   I don't think this can have

B1   because if there was nobody there that
            would be terrifying and if you were there

	that might be worse but it's something I wonder
SALTER	no
B1	could you hear me shouting?
SALTER	no I don't
B1	no
SALTER	no I don't think this happened in quite the
B1	what?
SALTER	because I'd
B1	again and again and again, every night I'd be
SALTER	no
B1	so you didn't hear?
SALTER	no but you can't have
B1	yes I was shouting, are you telling me you didn't
SALTER	no of course I didn't
B1	you didn't
SALTER	no
B1	you weren't sitting there listening to me shouting
SALTER	no
B1	you weren't out

SALTER   no

B1   so I needed to shout louder.

SALTER   Of course sometimes everyone who's had
            children will tell you sometimes you put
            them to bed and they want another story
            and you say goodnight now and go away
            and they call out once or twice and you
            say no go to sleep now and they might
            call out again and they go to sleep.

B1   The other one. Your son. My brother is
            he? my little twin.

SALTER   Yes.

B1   Has he got a child?

SALTER   No.

B1   Because if he had I'd kill it.

SALTER   No, he hasn't got one.

B1   So when you opened the door you didn't
            recognise me.

SALTER   No because

B1   Do you recognise me now?

SALTER   I know it's you.

B1   No but look at me.

SALTER   I have. I am.

B1   No, look in my eyes. No, keep looking.
            Look.

3

SALTER *and* BERNARD (B2).

B2	Not like me at all
SALTER	not like
B2	well like like but not identical not
SALTER	not identical no not
B2	because what struck me was how different
SALTER	yes I was struck
B2	you couldn't mistake
SALTER	no no not at all I knew at once it wasn't
B2	though of course he is older if I was older
SALTER	but even then you wouldn't
B2	I wouldn't be identical
SALTER	no no not at all no, you're a different
B2	just a bit like
SALTER	well bound to be a bit
B2	because for a start I'm not frightening.
SALTER	So what did he want did he

B2   no nothing really, not frightening not

SALTER   he didn't hit you?

B2   hit? god no, hit me? do you think?

SALTER   well he

B2   he could have done yes, no he shouted

SALTER   shouted

B1   shouted and rambled really, rambled he's
             not entirely

SALTER   no, well

B2   so that's what his childhood, his life, his
             childhood

SALTER   all kinds of

B2   has made him a nutter really is what I
             think I mean not a nutter but he's

SALTER   yes yes I'm not, yes he probably is.

B2   He says all kinds of wild

SALTER   yes

B2   so you don't know what to believe.

SALTER   And how did it end up, are you on
             friendly

B2   friendly no

SALTER   not

B2   no no we ended up

SALTER   yes

B2   we ended as I mean to go on with me
              running away, I was glad we were
              meeting in a public place, if I'd been at
              home you can't run away in your own
              home and if we'd been at his I wonder if
              he'd have let me go he might put me in
              a cupboard not really, anyway yes I got
              up and left and I kept thinking had he
              followed me.

SALTER   As you mean to go on as in not seeing
              him any more

B2   as in leaving the country.

SALTER   For what for a week or two a holiday, I
              don't

B2   leaving, going on yes I don't know, going
              away, I don't want to be here.

SALTER   But when you come back he'll still

B2   so maybe I won't

SALTER   but that's, not come back, no that's

B2   I don't know I don't know don't ask me
              I don't know. I'm going, I don't know. I
              don't want to be anywhere near him.

SALTER   You think he might try to hurt you?

B2   Why? why do you keep

SALTER   I don't know. Is it that?

B2   It's partly that, it's also it's horrible, I
              don't feel myself and there's the others

too, I don't want to see them I don't
want them

SALTER   I thought you did.

B2   I thought I did, I might, if I go away
by myself I might feel all right, I might
feel – you can understand that.

SALTER   Yes, yes I can.

B2   Because there's this person who's
identical to me

SALTER   he's not

B2   who's not identical, who's like

SALTER   not even very

B2   not very like but very something terrible
which is exactly the same genetic person

SALTER   not the same person

B2   and I don't like it.

SALTER   I know. I'm sorry.

B2   I know you're sorry I'm not

SALTER   I know

B2   I'm not trying to make you say sorry

SALTER   I know, I just am

B2   I know

SALTER   I just am sorry.

B2   He said some things.

SALTER   Yes.

B2   There's a lot of things I don't, could you
            tell me what happened to my mother?

SALTER   She's dead.

B2   Yes.

SALTER   I told you she was dead.

B2   Yes but she didn't die when I was born
            and she didn't die with the first child in
            a carcrash because the first child's not
            dead he's walking round the streets at
            night giving me nightmares. Unless she
            did die in a carcrash?

SALTER   No.

B2   No.

SALTER   Your mother, the thing a thing about
            your mother was that she wasn't very
            happy, she wasn't a very happy person at
            all, I don't mean there were sometimes
            days she wasn't happy or I did things
            that made her not happy I did of course,
            she was always not happy, often cheerful
            and

B2   she killed herself. How did she do that?

SALTER   She did it under a train under a tube
            train, she was one of those people when
            they say there has been a person under a
            train and the trains are delayed she was
            a person under a train.

B2	Were you with her?
SALTER	With her on the platform no, I was still *with* her more or less but not with her then no I was having a drink I think.
B2	And the boy?
SALTER	Do you know I don't remember where the boy was. I think he was at a friend's house, we had friends.
B2	And he was how old four?
SALTER	no no he was four later when I he was walking, about two just starting to talk
B2	he was four when you sent him
SALTER	that's right when his mother died he was two.
B2	So this was let me be clear this was before this was some years before I was born she died before
SALTER	yes
B2	so she was already always
SALTER	yes she was
B2	just so I'm clear. And then you and the boy you and your son
SALTER	we went on we just
B2	lived alone together
SALTER	yes

B2   you were bringing him up

SALTER   yes

B2   the best you could

SALTER   I

B2   until

SALTER   and my best wasn't very but I had my
            moments, don't think, I did cook meals
            now and then and read a story I'm sure
            I can remember a particularly boring
            and badly written little book about an
            elephant at sea. But I could have
            managed better.

B2   Yes he said something about it

SALTER   he said

B2   yes

SALTER   yes of course he did yes. I know I could
            have managed better because I did
            with you because I stopped, shut myself
            away, gave it all up came off it all while
            I waited for you and I think we may
            even have had that same book, maybe
            it's you I remember reading it to, do you
            remember it at all? it had an elephant
            in red trousers.

B2   No I don't think

SALTER   no it was terrible, we had far better
            books we had

B2   Maybe he shouldn't blame you, maybe it
              was a genetic, could you help drinking
              we don't know or drugs at the time
              philosophically as I understand it it
              wasn't viewed as not like now when our
              understanding's different and would a
              different person genetically different
              person not have been so been so
              vulnerable because there could always be
              some genetic addictive and then again
              someone with the same genetic exactly
              the same but at a different time a
              different cultural and of course all the
              personal all kinds of what happened in
              your own life your childhood or things
              all kind of because suppose you'd had a
              brother with identical an identical twin
              say but separated at birth so you had
              entirely different early you see what I'm
              saying would he have done the same
              things who can say he might have been
              a very loving father and in fact of course
              you have that in you to be that because
              you were to me so it's a combination of
              very complicated and that's who you
              were so probably I shouldn't blame you.

SALTER   I'd rather you blamed me. I blame
              myself.

B2   I'm not saying you weren't horrible.

SALTER   Couldn't I not have been?

B2   Apparently not.

SALTER   If I'd tried harder.

B2   But someone like you couldn't have tried
           harder. What does it mean? If you'd
           tried harder you'd have been different
           from what you were like and you weren't
           you were

SALTER   but then later I

B2   later yes

SALTER   I did try that's what I did I started again
           I

B2   that's what

SALTER   I was good I tried to be good I was good
           to you

B2   that's what you were like

SALTER   I was good

B2   but I can't you can't I can't give you
           credit for that if I don't give you blame
           for the other it's what you did it's what
           happened

SALTER   but it felt

B2   it felt

SALTER   it felt as if I tried I deliberately

B2   of course it felt

SALTER   well then

B2   it feels it always it feels doesn't it inside
           that's just how we feel what we are and

we don't know all these complicated we
can't know what we're it's too
complicated to disentangle all the causes
and we feel this is me I freely and of
course it's true who you are does freely
not forced by someone else but who you
are who you are itself forces or you'd be
someone else wouldn't you?

SALTER   I did some bad things. I deserve to
            suffer. I did some better things. I'd like
            recognition.

B2   That's how everyone feels, certainly.

SALTER   He still blames me.

B2   There's a difference then.

SALTER   You remind me of him.

B2   I remind myself of him. We both hate
            you.

SALTER   I thought you

B2   I don't blame you it's not your fault but
            what you've been like what you're like
            I can't help it.

SALTER   Yes of course.

B2   Except what he feels as hate and what
            I feel as hate are completely different
            because what you did to him and what
            you did to me are different things.

SALTER   I was nice to you.

B2   Yes you were.

SALTER   You don't have to go away. Not for long.

B2   It might make me feel better.

SALTER   I love you.

B2   That's something else you can't help.

SALTER   That's all right. That's all right.

B2   Also I'm afraid he'll kill me.

4

SALTER *and* BERNARD (B1).

SALTER   So what kind of a place was it? was it

B1   the place

SALTER   he was in a hotel was he or

B1   no

SALTER   I thought he was in a hotel. So where
               was he?

B1   what?

SALTER   I'm trying to get a picture.

B1   Does it matter?

SALTER   It won't bring him back no obviously but
               I'd like I'd like you can't help feeling
               curious you want to get at it and you're
               blocked in all directions, your son dies
               you want his body, you want to know
               where his body last was when he was
               alive, you can't help

B1   He had a room.

SALTER   In somebody's house, renting

B1   some small you know how the locals
               when you arrive, just a room not
               breakfast you'd go out for a coffee.

SALTER   So was it some pretty on a harbour front
           or

B1   no

SALTER   thinking of him on holiday

B1   in a street just a side

SALTER   but of course it wasn't a holiday he was
           hiding he thought he was hiding. Did
           you go inside the room?

B1   Just a small room, rather dark, one
           window and the shutters

SALTER   not very tidy I expect

B1   that's right, not tidy the bed not made,
           couple of books, bag on the floor with
           clothes half out of it

SALTER   did he scream?

B1   and you know what he's like, not tidy,
           am I tidy you don't know do you but
           you'd guess not wouldn't you but you'd
           be wrong there because I'm meticulous.

SALTER   What I want to know is how you
           actually, what you, how you got him to
           go off to some remote because that's
           what I'm imagining, you don't shoot the
           lodger without the landlady hearing, I
           don't know if you did shoot I don't know
           why I say shoot you could have had a
           knife you could have strangled, I can't
           think he would have gone off with you
           because he was frightened which is why

but perhaps you talked you made him
feel or did you follow him or lie in wait
in some dark? and I don't know how
you found him there did you follow him
from his house when he left or follow
him from here last time he?

B1   I didn't need to tell you it had happened

SALTER   but you did so naturally I want to

B1   and I'm wishing I hadn't

SALTER   no I'm glad

B1   and I'm not telling you

SALTER   because I won't tell anyone

B1   and there's nothing more to be said.

SALTER   What about the others? or is he the only
          one you hated because I loved him, I
          don't love the others, you and I have got
          common cause against the others don't
          forget, I'm still hoping we'll make our
          fortunes there. I'm going to talk to a
          solicitor, I've been too busy not busy but
          it's been like a storm going on I don't
          know what's gone on, it's not been very
          long ago it all started. You're not going
          to be a serial, wipe them all out so
          you're the only, back like it was at the
          start I'd understand that. If they do
          catch up with you, I'm sure they won't
          I'm sure you know what you're, if they
          do we'll tell them it was me it was my
          fault anyway you look at it. Don't you

agree, don't you feel that? Don't stop
talking to me. It wasn't his fault, you
should have killed me, it's my fault you.
Perhaps you're going to kill me, is that
why you've stopped talking? Shall I kill
myself? I'd do that for you if you like,
would you like that?

I'll tell you a thought, I could have killed
you and I didn't. I may have done
terrible things but I didn't kill you. I
could have killed you and had another
son, made one the same like I did or
start again have a different one get
married again and I didn't, I spared you
though you were this disgusting thing by
then anyone in their right mind would
have squashed you but I remembered
what you'd been like at the beginning
and I spared you, I didn't want a
different one, I wanted that again
because you were perfect just like that
and I loved you.

You know you asked me when you used
to shout in the night. Sometimes I was
there, I'd sit and listen to you or I'd not
be in any condition to hear you I'd just
be sitting. Sometimes I'd go out and
leave you. I don't think you got out
of bed, did you get out of bed, because
you'd be frightened what I'd do to you
so it was all right to go out. That was
just a short period you used to shout,
you grew out of that, you got so you'd

rather not see me, you wanted to be left
alone in the night, you wouldn't want
me to come any more. You'd nearly
stopped speaking do you remember that?
not speaking not eating I tried to make
you. I'd put you in the cupboard do you
remember? or I'd look for you
everywhere and I'd think you'd got away
and I'd find you under the bed. You
liked it there I'd put your dinner under
for you. But it got worse do you
remember? There was nobody but us.
One day I cleaned you up and said take
him into care. You didn't look too bad
and they took you away. My darling. Do
you remember that? Do you remember
that day because I don't remember it
you know. The whole thing is very vague
to me. It's two years I remember almost
nothing about but you must remember
things and when you're that age two
years is much longer, it wasn't very long
to me, it was one long night out. Can
you tell me anything you remember? the
day you left? can you tell me things I did
I might have forgotten?

B1   When I was following him there was a
            time I was getting on the same train and
            he looked round, I thought he was
            looking right at me but he didn't see me.
            I got on the train and went with him all
            the way.

SALTER   Yes? yes?

5

SALTER *and* MICHAEL BLACK, *his son, thirty-five.*

MICHAEL   Have you met the others?

SALTER   You're the first.

MICHAEL   Are you going to meet us all?

SALTER   I thought I'd start.

MICHAEL   I'm sure everyone will be pleased to meet you. I know I am.

SALTER   I'm sorry to stare.

MICHAEL   No, please, I can see it must be. Do I look like?

SALTER   Yes of course

MICHAEL   of course, I meant

SALTER   no no I didn't mean

MICHAEL   I suppose I meant how

SALTER   because of course you don't, you don't, not exactly

MICHAEL   no of course

SALTER   I wouldn't mistake

MICHAEL   no

SALTER   or I might at a casual

MICHAEL   of course

SALTER   but not if I really look

MICHAEL   no

SALTER   no

MICHAEL   because?

SALTER   because of the eyes. You don't look at
me in the same way.

MICHAEL   I'm looking at someone I don't know of
course.

SALTER   Maybe you could tell me a little

MICHAEL   about myself

SALTER   if you don't mind

MICHAEL   no of course, it's where to, you already
know I'm a teacher, mathematics, you
know I'm married, three children did I
tell you that

SALTER   yes but you didn't

MICHAEL   boy and girl twelve and eight and now a
baby well eighteen months so she's
walking and beginning to talk, I don't
have any photographs on me I didn't
think, there's no need for photographs is
there if you see someone all the time so

SALTER   are you happy?

MICHAEL   what now? or in general? Yes I think
I am, I don't think about it, I am. The

                  job gets me down sometimes. The
                  world's a mess of course. But you can't
                  help, a sunny morning, leaves turning,
                  off to the park with the baby, you can't
                  help feeling wonderful can you?

SALTER   Can't you?

MICHAEL   Well that's how I seem to be.

SALTER   Tell me. Forgive me

MICHAEL   no go on

SALTER   tell me something about yourself that's
                  really specific to you, something really
                  important

MICHAEL   what sort of?

SALTER   anything

MICHAEL   it's hard to

SALTER   yes.

MICHAEL   Well here's something I find fascinating,
                  there are these people who used to live
                  in holes in the ground, with all tunnels
                  and underground chambers and
                  sometimes you'd have a chamber you'd
                  get to it through a labyrinth of passages
                  and the ceiling got lower and lower so
                  you had to go on your hands and knees
                  and then wriggle on your stomach and
                  you'd get through to this chamber deep
                  deep down that had a hole like a
                  chimney like a well a hole all the way up
                  to the sky so you could sit in this

chamber this room this cave whatever
and look up at a little circle of sky going
past overhead. And when somebody died
they'd hollow out more little rooms so
they weren't buried underneath you they
were buried in the walls beside you. And
maybe sometimes they walled people up
alive in there, it's possible because of
how the remains were contorted but
either way of course they're dead by now
and very soon after they went in of
course. And

SALTER   I don't think this is what I'm looking for

MICHAEL   oh, how, sorry

SALTER   because what you're telling me is about
            something else and I was hoping for
            something about you

MICHAEL   I don't quite

SALTER   I'm sorry I don't know I was hoping

MICHAEL   you want what my beliefs, politics how
            I feel about war for instance is that?
            I dislike war, I'm not at all happy when
            people say we're doing a lot of good
            with our bombing, I'm never very
            comfortable with that. War's one of those
            things, don't you think, where everyone
            always thinks they're in the right have
            you noticed that? Nobody ever says
            we're the bad guys, we're going to beat
            shit out of the good guys. What do you
            think?

SALTER   I was hoping I don't know something more personal something from deep inside your life. If that's not intrusive.

MICHAEL   Maybe what maybe my wife's ears?

SALTER   Yes?

MICHAEL   Because last night we were watching the news and I thought what beautiful and slightly odd ears she's got, they're small but with big lobes, big relative to the small ear, and they're slightly pointy on top, like a disney elf or little animal ears and they're always there but you know how you suddenly notice and noticing that, I mean the way I love her, felt very felt what you said something deep inside. Or the children obviously, I could talk about, is this the sort of thing?

SALTER   it's not quite

MICHAEL   no

SALTER   because you're just describing other people or

MICHAEL   yes

SALTER   not yourself

MICHAEL   but it's people I love so

SALTER   it's not what I'm looking for. Because anyone could feel

MICHAEL   oh of course I'm not claiming

SALTER   I was somehow hoping

MICHAEL   yes

SALTER   further in

MICHAEL   yes

SALTER   just about yourself

MICHAEL   myself

SALTER   yes

MICHAEL   like maybe I'm lying in bed and it's
            comfortable and then it gets slightly not
            so comfortable and I move my legs or
            even turn over and then it's

SALTER   no

MICHAEL   no

SALTER   no that's

MICHAEL   yes that's something everyone

SALTER   yes

MICHAEL   well I don't know. I like blue socks.
            Banana icecream. Does that help you?

SALTER   Dogs?

MICHAEL   do I like

SALTER   dogs

MICHAEL   I'm ok with dogs. My daughter wants a
            puppy but I don't know. Is dogs the kind
            of thing?

SALTER   So tell me what did you feel when you found out?

MICHAEL   Fascinated.

SALTER   Not angry?

MICHAEL   No.

SALTER   Not frightened.

MICHAEL   No, what of?

SALTER   Your life, losing your life.

MICHAEL   I've still got my life.

SALTER   But there are things there are things that are what you are, I think you're avoiding

MICHAEL   yes perhaps

SALTER   because then you might be frightened

MICHAEL   I don't think

SALTER   or angry

MICHAEL   not really

SALTER   because what does it do what does it to you to everything if there are all these walking around, what it does to me what am I and it's not even me it happened to, so how you can just, you must think something about it.

MICHAEL   I think it's funny, I think it's delightful

SALTER   delightful?

MICHAEL   all these very similar people doing things
            like each other or a bit different or
            whatever we're doing, what a thrill for
            the mad old professor if he'd lived to see
            it, I do see the joy of it. I know you're
            not at all happy.

SALTER   I didn't feel I'd lost him when I sent him
            away because I had the second chance.
            And when the second one my son the
            second son was murdered it wasn't so
            bad as you'd think because it seemed
            fair. I was back with the first one.

MICHAEL   But now

SALTER   now he's killed himself

MICHAEL   now you feel

SALTER   now I've lost him, I've lost

MICHAEL   yes

SALTER   now I can't put it right any more.
            Because the second time round you see I
            slept very lightly with the door open.

MICHAEL   Is that the worst you did, not go in the
            night?

SALTER   No of course not.

MICHAEL   Like what?

SALTER   Things that are what I did that are not
            trivial like banana icecream nor
            unifuckingversal like turning over in bed.

MICHAEL   We've got ninety-nine per cent the same
           genes as any other person. We've got
           ninety per cent the same as a chimpanzee.
           We've got thirty percent the same as a
           lettuce. Does that cheer you up at all?
           I love about the lettuce. It makes me feel
           I belong.

SALTER   I miss him so much. I miss them both.

MICHAEL   There's nineteen more of us.

SALTER   That's not the same.

MICHAEL   No of course not. I was making a joke.

SALTER   And you're happy you say are you? you
           like your life?

MICHAEL   I do yes, sorry.

A Nick Hern Book

A Number first published in 2002 as a paperback original
by Nick Hern Books, 14 Larden Road, London W3 7ST
in association with the Royal Court Theatre

A Number copyright © 2002 by Caryl Churchill Ltd

Caryl Churchill has asserted her right to be identified
as the author of this work

Typeset by Country Setting, Kingsdown, Kent, CT14 8ES
Printed in Great Britain by Bookmarque, Croydon, Surrey

ISBN 1 8545 709 4

A CIP catalogue record for this book is available
from the British Library